15295

# GRASSLANDS

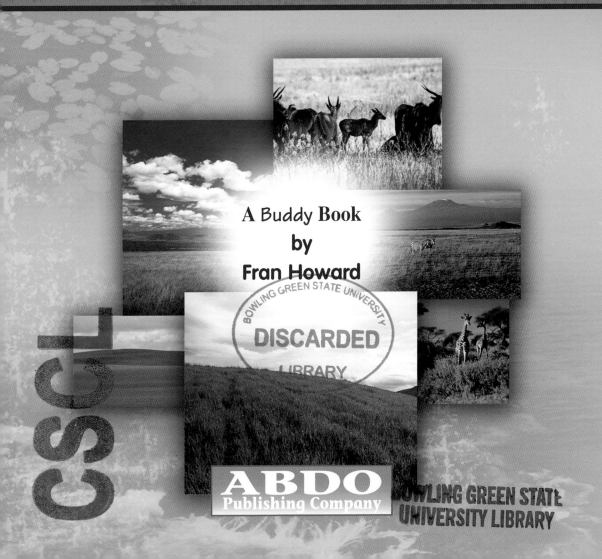

A Buddy Book
by
Fran Howard

**ABDO**
Publishing Company

## VISIT US AT
www.abdopublishing.com

Published by ABDO Publishing Company, 4940 Viking Drive, Edina, Minnesota 55435.

Printed in the United States.

Edited by: Sarah Tieck
Contributing Editor: Michael P. Goecke
Graphic Design: Brady Wise
Image Research: Deb Coldiron, Maria Hosley, Heather Sagisser, Brady Wise
Photographs: Maynard Agena, photos.com, Superstock

## Library of Congress Cataloging-in-Publication Data

Howard, Fran, 1953-
    Grasslands / Fran Howard.
       p. cm. — (Habitats)
    Includes bibliographical references and index.
    ISBN 1-59679-778-9 (10 digit ISBN)
    ISBN 978-1-59679-778-9 (13 digit ISBN)
       1. Grasslands—Juvenile literature. I. Title. II. Series: Habitats (Edina, Minn.)

QH87.7.H69 2006
577.4—dc22

                                                2005031599

# TABLE OF CONTENTS

# What Is A Grassland?

When people think of grasslands, they think of wide-open spaces.

Grasslands are large land areas covered with grass. Grasses, flowers, and herbs all grow in grasslands.

A grassland is one kind of habitat. Habitats are the places where plants and animals find food, water, and places to live. Different plants and animals live in different habitats.

Grasslands can be windy places. They are drier than forests. But, they are not as dry as deserts.

# WHERE ARE GRASSLANDS FOUND?

Today, grasslands cover about one-quarter of the Earth. There used to be more grasslands. That land is now used for other things. Some people have turned grasslands into farms or ranches.

Farmers plant crops such as wheat on grasslands. Growing crops changes grasslands.

There are different types of grasslands throughout the world.

# LIFE ON A PRAIRIE

A prairie in north-central Iowa.

A prairie is one type of grassland. Prairies are found in North America, Europe, and Asia. Prairies have both cold and warm weather.

Prairies have short and tall grasses. Some grass grows taller than a small child. It can be as much as five feet (two m) tall. Prairie grass is very strong. It covers most of the soil.

Tough prairie grasses can survive strong winds and grow in water.

Blooming prairie flowers

Colorful wildflowers bloom on prairies in the spring and summer. The weather is warm during these months.

Prairie flowers come in many different colors.

Many of the animals that live on prairies eat plants. Bugs often eat grasses. Some birds, such as meadowlarks, eat the grass seed.

Eastern meadowlarks

A bison

Some **mammals** eat grass, too. Rabbits, prairie dogs, and mice all eat grass. Bison spend most of the day eating grass. They are one of the largest animals found on prairies.

# LIFE ON A SAVANNA

Savannas are another type of grassland. These are found in Africa, Australia, Asia, and South America.

The weather is hot in most savannas. Some savannas are very dry. Dry savannas have very short grass.

Some savannas are known for short grasses.

Some savannas can get as much as 60 inches (150 cm) of rain each year. Rain helps new grass to grow. These savannas have very tall grass. This grass can be 10 feet (3 m) tall. This is almost twice as tall as an adult person!

This tree is growing on a savanna.

Grass on a savanna grows in clumps. It does not cover all the dirt. Savannas have trees and shrubs, too. They don't have as many as a forest, though.

Many large animals that live on savannas eat plants. Zebras, kangaroos, and elephants eat grasses. Elephants and giraffes eat leaves from the trees and bushes. Elephants use their trunks to pull down tree branches. A giraffe's long neck helps it reach the treetops.

Elephants (below) and giraffes (right) graze in grasslands.

# GRASSLAND
# PREDATORS

Coyotes hunt prey in grasslands.

Some animals hunt and eat other animals. These animals are called **carnivores**. Many carnivores are also **predators**. Many predators live on prairies and savannas.

Eagles are prairie predators.

Badgers are **predators** of the prairie. They hunt rodents. Rodents hide in **burrows**. Badgers have sharp claws and are good diggers. They can dig rodents out of their burrows.

A badger

A cheetah

Lions, leopards, and cheetahs are **predators** of the savanna. Lions hunt in groups. Leopards are good climbers. Cheetahs chase their **prey**. Some cheetahs run as fast as 60 miles (97 km) per hour!

A lion

A leopard

# Why Are Grassland Habitats IMPORTANT?

Grassland animals and plants need each other. Together they form a **food chain**. Even the smallest plants and animals are part of this chain.

Badger

Mouse

Grass

Tall grasses help animals hide from predators.

Grasslands supply food and shelter for many animals. They also help provide food for people.

Many people have farms on prairies. They raise different kinds of food on farms.

Prairies are known for having dark, rich soil. Rich prairie soil is created from rotting plants. It is full of nutrients that help other plants and grasses grow.

This is a farm in Iowa. Some of its land is used to grow prairie grasses and native flowers. This helps the land become more fertile.

Some grasslands have been turned into parks. This protects the grassland habitat. Grassland plants and animals cannot live without their habitat.

# GRASSLANDS

- Fires are common in grasslands. The first lightning strikes of the rainy season often set the grass on fire.

- Temperatures in prairies can drop more than 100°F (38°C) from summer to winter.

- The United States has 20 National Grasslands.

- Elephants are the largest animals on the African savanna. Males can weigh more than seven tons (six t) and eat more than 300 pounds (140 kg) of food in one day.

- By 1890, hunters had killed almost all of the bison in North America's grasslands. It is estimated that only 1,000 bison were alive in 1890.

# Important Words

burrow  a tunnel or hole in the ground where some animals live.

carnivore  an animal that eats meat.

food chain  the order in which plants and animals feed on each other.

mammal  most living things that belong to this special group have hair, give birth to live babies, and make milk to feed their babies.

predator  an animal that hunts other animals.

prey  an animal that is hunted by another animal.

# Web Sites

# INDEX